I0446213

THE HIDDEN PATH TO BUSINESS SUCCESS

SIMPLE SECRETS FOR A SUCCESSFUL BUSINESS

By STANLEY BLAISE

Table of contents

THE HIDDEN PATH TO BUSINESS SUCCESS

CHAPTER 1: BUSINESS INSIGHT FOR EXPLOITS

CHAPTER 2: LOVING GOD

CHAPTER 3: KINGDOM DREAM FOR BUSINESS EXPLOITS

CHAPTER 4: ADVICE FOR BUSINESS EXPLOITS

CHAPTER 5: ACCESS THE AVAILABLE

CHAPTER 6: HOW TO START BUSINESS WITHOUT MONEY

CHAPTER 7: USEFUL TIPS FOR BUSINESS EXPLOITS

CHAPTER 8: OUTSTANDING CUSTOMER SERVICE

CHAPTER 9: ACHIEVE PROGRESS

THE HIDDEN PATH TO BUSINESS SUCCESS

THE HIDDEN PATH TO BUSINESS SUCCESS

INTRODUCTION

Certain elements improve business safety and profitability. When you gather these elements and start using them, your firm stands out.

Happy are you if you follow these instructions if you know them.
John 13:17

A business covenant practitioner is required to get business insurance. By ensuring stability, safety, and viability, this insurance helps. It is a fallback provided by God. For instance, your tithe shields your company from the devourer's meddling. Your tithe is an appeal to God Almighty to be actively involved in your business and to guard it. Your company may flourish and achieve fame. Because God is engaged, it has the potential to set a new standard. Isaiah 3:8–12

In business, diligence is a factor that ensures success. Your attitude in the workplace affects your height. In life and business, there is no great outcome without a dent of hard labour. Being idle is a devilish plot to drag you into a miserable life. You weren't made to just sit around. You are designed to succeed at work.

One quality that sets you apart in business is faithfulness. Your commitment to your business will always result in success there. Never play honorably. Being unfaithful might lead to unusual loss.

.The person who had gotten the five talents then returned with another five, saying, "Lord, you gave me five talents; look at the five talents I've gained in addition to them." Well done, good and faithful servant; for being faithful over a few things, I will appoint thee ruler over many things; enter into the joy of thy master, his lord replied to him. 20–21 in Matthew 25

The provisions of covenant insurance, faithfulness, and diligence must be used by those who want to succeed in business.

By God's grace, our current situation is a result of having a kingdom dream. You are prepared for adventures once you have a vision of your future.

Other things like being a benefit to others and having a love for service can also help you succeed in business. Our deeds demonstrate our fervour for God's kingdom and the welfare of people.

Relevant information is necessary if you want to perform at your very best in business. Nothing to exploit, nothing to know. Your greatest asset in business is learning the necessary information. You will be unusually distorted in business if you are not aware. To move quickly in life and business, you need facts.

And you will come to know the truth, which will set you free. John 8:3

A businessman can become renowned through information. Business stagnation is a result of a lack of information. A company that lacks important information has no colour. Now is the moment to look for business information that will inspire your venture. When you are lacking pertinent information, it is impossible to do business with excellence. We'll wrap up our discussion by showing you how to launch a business without any funding. It is not insurmountable! All you need is a solid plan and the motivation to implement it. Wisdom was the only component necessary for the universe to be created. The foundation for exploits is wisdom.

Finally, you must make advantage of what is offered. Your exploit is guaranteed when you are aware of what is in your possession and use it. Create what you want using the resources you already have. The life of our covenant father, Abraham, has some insightful business advice: you must identify with God; have a vision; be hardworking; be a donor; have faith; and be content with your resources.

Customer service that is efficient and effective will guarantee successful business outcomes. Good customer service will help your business grow.

Be resolved to make progress more procrastination using all the knowledge you will learn from this book.

Expand the area of your tent and allow them to extend the curtains of your homes; do not skimp on the length of your poles; for you will split off on the right and left, and your progeny will inherit the Gentiles and bring life to the deserted towns.
Isa. 54:2–3.

Start small and gradually expand your coast.

CHAPTER 1: BUSINESS INSIGHT FOR EXPLOITS

A value exchange that benefits both parties engaged is what is meant by the term "business." It is a for-profit business. The capacity for business is to grow resources and advance.

Like breeds, that much is evident. God does not fall short. This indicates that because you are like God, you are not a failure from birth. Everyone who is born of God has a huge endowment that makes them eligible to start a successful business. You cannot reside among the humble since God (our Father) is the Most High God. You are not mediocre by birth; you belong at the top. Every star is radiant. No star can prevent another from shining, therefore everyone in the kingdom has a chance to shine.

Jesus said to "occupy until I come" (Luke 19:13) and offered each man a variety of skills (Matthew 25:14–30). That means that until Jesus returns, everyone should be working on something. There is a fundamental reality about business that cannot be overlooked. There is no way to be successful in business without that. It is known as Wisdom. Without wisdom, it is impossible to be successful in business.

The person who discovers wisdom and acquires comprehension is happy.

Because its goods are superior to those of silver and its profits to those of excellent gold.
She is more valuable than rubies, and all you could possibly want is incomparable to her.
In her right band is the number of days, and in her left band are riches and honour.
Proverbs 3:13–16

Business wealth and exploitation are the results of wisdom. Therefore, it is wise to seek wisdom before seeking wealth, success, and achievements in your business.

When you have wisdom, your business endeavours reach a fantastic level. Being wise will help you make money. When resources are available but intelligence is absent, failure is unavoidable and progress cannot be made.

A breakthrough is primarily determined by divine knowledge. It is wealth's commander. If the goal of the company is to maximise profits, wisdom is your most important business asset.

The first thing you should ask from God is wisdom.
And God said unto him, Because thou bast asked this thing, and hast not asked for thyself long life; neither bast asked riches for thyself... but bast asked for thyself understanding to discern judgment;

o Bebold, I have done according to thy words: lo, I have given thee a wise and an understanding heart; so that there was none like thee before thee, neither after thee shall any arise like unto thee.

And I have also given thee that which thou bast not asked, both riches and honor: so that there shall not be any among the kings like unto thee all thy
days.
1 Kings 3:11-13

Solomon never asked for wealth; he asked for wisdom. It was wisdom that guaranteed the other additional things that came. If you want God to favor you with exploits in your business, ask Him for
wisdom

To the only wise God our Saviour, be glory and majesty, dominion and power, both now and ever. Amen.
Jude 1:25

If God is the only wise God, then you (as His child) should be the only wise one among your peers in that business. Everything in this world came to be, as a function of the display of God's wisdom. It therefore means, if God (by wisdom) did exploits, you too by wisdom should follow suit. It is the wisdom of God that guarantees exploitation in business and whatsoever you are doing.

Therefore whosoever heareth these sayings of mine, and doeth them, I will liken him unto a wise man, which built bis bouse upon a rock:
And the rain descended, and the floods came, and the winds blew, and beat upon that house; and it fell not: for it was founded upon a rock. And every one that heareth these sayings of mine, and doeth them not, shall be likened unto a foolish man, which built bis bouse upon the sand: And the rain descended, and the floods came, and the winds blew, and

beat upon that house; and it fell: and great
was the fall of it.
Matthew 7:24-27

When you hearken to God's word and obey
promptly, you are wise. God will lavish you
with undeniable and impeccable wisdom.
Irrespective of the challenging Circumstance
yOu face in your business,
you will see yourself triumphing over it.
Wisdom is complying with the demands of
scriptures in your approach to your business.

And it shall come to pass, if thou shalt
hearken diligently unto the voice of the
LORD thy God, to observe and to do all bis
commandments which I command thee this
day, that the LORD thy God will set thee on
high above all nations of the earth...
And the LORD shall make thee the bead,
and not the tail; and thou shalt be above only,

and thou shalt not be beneath; if that thou hearken unto the commandments of the LORD thy God, which I command thee this day, to observe and to do them:
Deuteronomy 28:1,13

When you observe to do whatever God tells you to do concerning your business, you are operating in wisdom. Once your obedience is in place, exploits in business are Sure.

There are three major factors that guarantee business exploits:
1. You must ensure that business The first thing for you to do in business is to sign a Covenant Insurance Policy. It is what will enhance the safety and profitability of your business.
Except the LORD build the bouse, they labor in vain that build it: except the LORD keep the city, the watchman waketh but in vain.

Psalm 127:1

God is the only Source of stability in your business. His blessing (being your avenue of exploits) makes you rich without any iota of sorrow attached to it- Proverbs 10:22. You cannot be successful in business without backup from God.

Covenant insurance policy begins with tithing. As a Christian, you must not Ignore paying your tithe. When you do this you create room for the devourer to penetrate. When you pay tithe, you are saturated with business ideas that will guarantee your exploit.

Will a man rob God? Yet ye have robbed me. But ye say, Wherein have we robbed thee? In tithes and offerings.
Ye are cursed with a curse: for ye have robbed me, even this whole nation.

Bring ye all the tithes into the storehouse, that there may be meat in mine house, and prove me now herewith, saith the LORD of hosts, if I will not open you the windows of heaven, and pour you
pour you out a blessing, that there shall not be
room enough to receive it. And I will rebuke the devourer for your sakes, and he shall not destroy the fruits of your ground; neither shall your vine cast her fruit before the time in the field, saith the LORD of hosts. And all nations shall call you blessed: for ye shall be a delightsome land, saith the LORD of hosts.
Malachi 3:8-11

God said He would rebuke the devourer. This can only come through when you pay your tithe faithfully. Your business is insured and protected first through tithing. Hence, be tithing conscious in your business.

Our church pays tithe that is why God gets involved in the business of rebuking every devourer and giving us all round victory. Beyond paying your tithes, also give for "kingdom investments". It is equally important.

2. You must be diligent

Seest thou a man diligent in bis business? he shall stand before kings; he shall not stand before
mean men.
Proverbs 22:2

Business breakthrough is impossible without diligence. In all labor there is profit... Proverbs 14:23. Profiting is connected to labor. There is no future for an idle man, not even in the kingdom of God. Idleness is an instrument of decay. A building that is not used will deteriorate. Be diligent if you want to exploit business. Breakthrough does not answer to desires, it answers to your diligence.

3. You must be faithful

A faithful man shall abound with blessings: but he that maketh haste to be rich shall not be innocent.
Proverbs 28:20

Breakthrough and exploitation in business demands faithfulness./If you are not faithful, you cannot be fruitful. Integrity in business qualifies you for great prosperity.

Jesus cited an instance where some servants were entrusted with money to trade with, to test their faithfulness Matthew 25:14-30. When their master returned from his journey, one was found unfaithful; he did not trade with the money he was given. He lost his reward and was punished for that act. Unfaithfulness can lead to condemnation.

If therefore ye have not been faithful in the unrighteous mammon, who will commit to your trust the true riches?
Luke 16:11

Unfaithfulness is a thief of trust. If you are not faithful in money, God will not commit to you true riches.

These three factors are vital tools in business. The exploit is impossible without adhering to these three things.

CHAPTER 2: LOVING GOD

In the kingdom of God, there is a foundation for long-lasting successes. Love for God is the basis of this.

This is the first commandment: "And thou shalt love the Lord thy God with all thy heart, with all thy soul, with all thy mind, and with all thy strength."
Mark 12:30

According to Psalm 11:3, if you undermine the foundation, no exploits will ever be accomplished. Before you may have permanent victories on earth, you must have a love for God. Your birthright is exploitation, but the road to it is via God's love. Every biblical precept interacts with the precept of love for God. Use what people admire and respect about you to love God.

But put God's kingdom and righteousness first, and everything else will be added to you (Matthew 6:33).

Anything you desire above God has already limited you; similarly, anything you cherish above God turns you into an idolater since idolatry is the act of putting something above God.

Love is the first step on the path to enduring victories with God.

Solomon loved the LORD and followed the rules established by his father, King David, save that he offered sacrifices and burned incense on holy places. Gibeon was a great high place, therefore the king travelled there to make sacrifices.

Solomon offered a thousand burned offerings on that altar. There was no one like you before, and there won't be anybody like you after, for I have done as I promised: see, I have given you a knowledgeable and discerning heart. There won't be another monarch like you for the rest of your days because I also gave you the riches and honour you didn't ask for.
1 Kings 3:3-4,12-13

In his day, Solomon was the richest man, and he cherished the Lord, his God. Solomon's access to wealth resulted from his love for

God, not from a desire for money. Without a deep-seated love for God, attending church and giving to His kingdom would only make you frustrated. Giving without a passion for God will quickly make you exhausted. Your position in the kingdom depends on how much you love God.

Your ability to draw from divine resources increases with the depth of your love. God cannot be loved by anyone who does not give to Him selflessly. God gave selflessly as a sign of His love for people.

Because God loved the world so much, he gave his only Son, ensuring that everyone who trusted in him would not perish but instead experience eternal life.
John 3:16

Knowing God allows you to give, but loving God causes you to sow selflessly. God must reply if your offering is motivated by love. Giving inspired by love, is distinct.

During my research, I found that every person God blessed in the Bible was a giver. Before God benefited them, they sowed to Him. This is so that God can gauge how generous you are before blessing you. He will first see if you are "free-handed" so that when He provides you, you will advance His kingdom.

Abraham loved God, and because of his kindness, God blessed him with prosperity.

EVIDENCE THAT YOU LOVE GOD

1. A DEVOTION TO HIS WORD

How much I adore your law! My daily
meditation is doing that.
Psalm 119:97

Then, because my Father loves him, we will
come to him and establish our abode with
him, Jesus said, "If a man loves me, he will
keep my words."
John 14:23

You will adore the Bible if you claim to love
God. If you love God, you won't fall asleep
while listening to the sermon. Some attendees
in the church doze off during the sermon.
Any man who loves God will enjoy hearing
God's word.

My greatest secret is my love for God, which
is what makes things go well. It serves as my

destiny's mooring. You must first love God before you may access my secrets.

2. LOVE FOR HIS HOUSE

How pleasant are your tabernacles, O LORD of hosts; My soul longs, yea, even faints for the courts of the LORD; my heart and my flesh cry out for the living God; For a day in thy courts is better than a thousand; I would rather be a doorkeeper in thy house than dwell in the tents of wickedness. Psalm 84:1-2,10

Have there ever been times when you felt uneasy at home and yearned to leave for church? You can identify those who cherish His home by doing so. You have a problem if they announce there is no service and you respond, "Thank God."

3. You'll respect His directives

You will not challenge whatever God says. He who keeps my commands is the one who loves me; he who loves me will be loved by my Father, and I will love him and make my presence known to him.
John 14:21

When God turned to face Abraham, he declared, "He is a man that loves me"! As soon as you begin to love Him, you will obey if He gives you a command. People who love God accept everything He says.

4. YOU'LL ADORE ADVANCING HIS KINGDOM.

The LORD of hosts so declares, "This people claim that the proper time for the construction of the LORD's temple has not yet arrived."

Then Haggai the prophet spoke for the LORD and asked: "Is it time for you, O you, to dwell in your cemented houses, and this house lie waste?"

Because of this, the LORD of hosts says, "Consider your Ways."

You sow a lot but harvest little; you eat but do not have enough; you drink but are not satisfied; you dress but there is no one to keep you warm; and the only person earning money stuffs it into a sack with holes.

So says the LORD of the bosts: Think about your actions.

I will enjoy it and I will be honoured, says the LORD, so go up the mountain, bring wood, and build the house.

Haggai 1:2–8

If you love God, you will be involved in advancing the kingdom of God. You simply promote the kingdom of God because you genuinely love God; you won't wait for an invitation or a request.

5. YOU'LL ADORE WINNING SOULS.

Because God loved the world so much, he gave his only Son, ensuring that everyone who trusted in him would not perish but instead experience eternal life.
John 3:16

You will love sinners and lead them to Jesus if you love God. I cannot claim to love God and not engage in soul-winning.

6: YOU'LL CHERISH YOUR NEIGHBOURS.

He who claims to love God while harbouring hatred for his brother is lying because he cannot love God, whose he has not seen, if he does not also love his brother.
And he gave us the instruction that whoever loves God must also love his neighbour.
1 John 4:20-21

If you were born again, love is already present in you.

The Holy Ghost, who is given to Us, causes the love of God to be diffused abroad in our hearts.
Romans 5:5

Because God has already shed that love in your heart, all you need to do is express it.

Anyone who loves Him has something in store for them (1 Corinthians 2:9). In the name of Jesus, may the best of God be given to you as you follow his instructions. When you gain God's affection, He gives His finest to you. Love is not mechanical; it emanates from the heart. You will be aware if you adore God.

CHAPTER 3: KINGDOM DREAM FOR BUSINESS EXPLOITS

The "future picture" of a desirable tomorrow in accordance with God's word is known as a kingdom dream. By using God's word, you can glimpse what lies ahead before you ever dream it.
The days of adventures are upon us.

And it will happen in the last days that the mountain of the LORD's house will be constructed above mountains, elevated above hills, and will draw people from all over the world.

Isaiah 2:2

God promises that in the end days, we will
use our authority to produce extraordinary
and admirable achievements that will astound
everyone. they will then give themselves over
to serving God. God isn't just concerned with
your spiritual life; He's also concerned with
your career.

Dearest, I want nothing more than for you to
prosper and be healthy, just as your soul
does.
3 John 1:2

God desires for you to prosper in business.

And if thou shalt carefully obey the voice of
the LORD thy God, keeping in mind and
carrying out all his commands which I give

thee this day, the LORD thy God shall exalt
thee above all peoples of the earth:
Deuteronomy 28: 1

You will be exalted if you obey God's
instructions.

God has no regard for human rights. You are
eligible to take use of His promises once you
have obeyed His order to the letter. I am
aware of this and have walked in accordance
with His instructions. That is why God
favours me beyond my wildest dreams in
every country in the world.

Because he is what he believes to be in his
heart...
Psalms 23:7

Never let your thoughts conflict with God's
assurances for your life.

There are a few things that give you the advantage in business, including:

1.BLESSED TO BE A BLESSING

You are eligible for God's blessings because you aspire to be a blessing. Until you are prepared to be a blessing, God will not grant you a breakthrough.

And I'll bless you, create you a big nation, and elevate your name so that you become a blessing: Genesis 12:2

Even strangers received blessings from Abraham. (Genesis 14:14) Abraham had 318 people working for him. One guy was the main employer of labour if he had 3 18 trained employees. He was in charge of managing the economy at the time. Because he was prepared to be a blessing, he was the keeper of power and authority as well as a prominent member of society.

God will never give you the breakthrough power you need unless you are prepared to benefit others.

Charge those who are wealthy in this world to not be proud or put their reliance in speculative wealth, but rather in the living God who abundantly provides for all our needs; that they are excellent people who have done a lot of good deeds and are prepared to share and communicate;
Timotheus 1:17–18

Be willing to share if you want God to give your business an extraordinary growth spurt. Your business expands the more you distribute. No great man ever rose to greatness by focusing only on himself.

Without a dream, one is doomed. The extent of your lifting is thus determined by how big your heart and your dream are for God's kingdom. Stop obsessing on your own interests.

2. HAVE A SACRED PASSION

You should adopt the same mindset that Christ Jesus did:
Who, while taking the form of God, did not consider it theft to be on par with God:
However, he became a nobody, assumed the appearance of a servant, and was created in the image of a man:
And after being accepted as a man, he debased himself and submitted to death—even the death on a cross.
Because of this, God has also greatly exalted him and given him the name that is beyond all names: 2:5–9 in Philippians

He made himself into a nobody. He was prepared to help people.

Be prepared to serve humanity if you want your business to succeed. Instead of pursuing acquisition, seek giving. Find out what you can do to influence your community. Life is not dependent on how long it lasts, but rather on how much you give to others, or how much of yourself you put into the world.

And word of his reputation spread widely throughout the entire nation.
Luke 4:37

The impact of Jesus on the globe is still felt today. Consider what you can do to improve the planet.
Jesus lived for everyone when He arrived on earth. Even when God decided to chastise the Israelites, Moses came and lived for them,

pleading for God to have mercy on them. Paul also became quite passionate about serving God in a way that is acceptable. Even after they have passed away, these men are still remembered for what they had done. What contribution have I made that the world will remember me for, you ask? I implore you to have a righteous zeal for God's kingdom and His people as a Christian.

A problem you can tackle is indicated by your desire. People lack passion, which renders them helpless. What has propelled me this far is my fervent love for God and His people. Because I am pleasing to God, He has anointed me beyond my wildest dreams and to the envy of others. We have an enormous congregation, which is a blessing from God. Why? Passion! If you want God's support, be fervent about His things.

And they will rebuild the ancient wastelands, restore the earlier desolation, and restore the abandoned cities, which have been destroyed for many centuries.
Foreigners' sons will work as your ploughmen and vinedressers, and strangers will stand and feed your sheep.
Isaiah 61:4–5.

Anointing is more of a love and passion for humanity than just a result of fasting and prayer. For instance, if you do not have a burning desire to help the needy, God cannot anoint you for money. A conservative Christian won't be blessed with wealth. If you are not a blessing to humanity, people will start to doubt your Christianity. God will grow disappointed in you.

And I'll bless you and exalt your name, making you a blessing in the world:

Genesis 12:2

Your success is related to your fervour for God's kingdom and the emancipation of humanity. Those who live independently in God's kingdom are rife with foolishness; on the other hand, you are a wise man. Consider what you can do for humanity.

Many businessmen struggle because they lack a Kingdom Dream. If you want to be successful in life and business, have a kingdom dream. When you personally pay your tithe and make sure that your organisation (business) likewise pays tithe, your kingdom dream will begin to come true. Do not think that by paying tithes, you are assisting God. It might have a negative impact on your life and business.

But put God's kingdom and righteousness first, and everything else will be added to you. Matthew 6: 33

You'll be able to see God's hand at work in your life and business if you first seek the kingdom.
In the name of Jesus, all your dreams that are in accordance with God's word will come true.

CHAPTER 4: ADVICE FOR BUSINESS EXPLOITS

You cannot succeed without knowledge. The key to success in today's environment is knowledge. There are individuals working in a variety of businesses nowadays who are just aware of their own personal opinions. Your personal notion won't get you where you want to go in life or business. To advance, you need to combine someone else's concept with your own. Whatever you are doing right now, someone else has already done it. There is nothing new under the sun.

In order to enhance your own ideas, you must be aware of what others have accomplished. Being overweight requires fact. Facts are necessary if you wish to stand out in any sphere of endeavour.

Finding information and using them effectively will help you succeed in life.

Being prosperous means knowing what to do at each moment to control events and profit from whatever endeavour you are engaged in. Luck is a myth that only the ignorant hold. Men of substance trust in the truth.

Any business is developed by careful planning, strengthened through common sense, and profitably by staying up to date with the facts.
Proverbs 24:3–4 (TLB)

Plan ahead if you want to be successful and outstanding. The information you need to get to where you belong in life is included in the facts you gather about your company.

Every successful person in the world today came into contact with some sort of information that helped them succeed.

I recently read about Richard Branson, the man who started Virgin Airlines. "Small is Beautiful" is a book that Richard Branson found. At sixteen (16), he stopped attending school. He started selling newspapers in London. He read that book and learned some important facts from it. He put the knowledge to use, which completely changed his life and made him a billionaire.To convert requires information. You cannot change until you are informed. Lack of knowledge distorts. Until you are fully informed, you cannot achieve or prosper in everything you undertake.

A young guy won the long jump gold medal in the 1936 Olympics. He asked his coach what it takes to be a great man in sports before the event to find out. He had straightforward information to work with from his coach. He was advised that in order to succeed, he would need these four qualities: resolve, commitment, assiduity, and discipline. The young man resolved to use that knowledge to improve himself after accepting it. He ascended to greater heights in life and rose to fame.

It is an idea that creates the ideal circumstance you seek in life. You succeed in life via knowledge, not luck or magic. Your ultimate transformation in life depends on the worth of the knowledge you gain. Your ability to make informed decisions will affect the outcome. You actively seek out knowledge rather than waiting for it. You will undoubtedly achieve better results when you apply superior information. Proper information is essential for resounding achievement. If you put effort into it, it will work for you.

For instance, "change" is necessary if the church, the body of Christ, is to have an impact on the world. The Church must reject being caught up in tradition and religion and shun dogmatism. Any alteration that may hasten the church's development or expansion must be accommodated. It is quite surprising how certain churches have purposefully refused to change and continue to operate in the same manner! They operate by the principle "as it was in the beginning, so it will be."The church must seek out important information and adjust to change if it is to enjoy rapid worldwide impact, dominion, and relevance. Every company unit, according to a wise man, must function like a biological nervous system with the capacity to integrate information into various sources so that prompt judgements can be made.

Stop waiting! Do something about your life; seek for information. Lack of information multiplies a challenge and eliminates solutions to that challenge. Even as a pastor, you must go for information to add flavor to your preaching - do not make your preaching look archaic. Do not use prayer and fasting as a substitute for information. Let there be a touch of excellence in how you conduct service. As a pastor, if you do not know the name of the Presiding Pastor of the largest congregation in the world, you lack information. If you have not read any book on church growth, church administration, and management, you lack information. If you experience stagnation in your ministry, do not blame the devil; just know that what the scripture says in Hosea 4:6 applies to you. "My people are destroyed for lack of knowledge..." As a result of this, God also said: "...because thou hast rejected knowledge, I will also reject thee... " Hosea 4:6. That divine assignment God had placed in your hand requires continuous and appropriate information if you must succeed. Study the Bible, and other books by proven anointed authors, and take note of good things which can add value to your ministry if you are diligent to implement them. Information and sensitivity are imperative in your business or assignment if you must arrive at the top. Go for information and be sensitive to how you can apply what you have learned to achieve your desired result.

If you read the account of our Lord Jesus Christ in Luke 4, you will discover He considered information as a vital tool for progress; and that caused His fame to spread abroad. If He did it then you cannot be exempted from acquiring knowledge. Whether in your career, profession, business, family, etc.; to be outstanding in life, you need information. Do not neglect it.

CHAPTER 5: ACCESS THE AVAILABLE

Everything that God wants to use to boost and bless you is all around you. God won't raise you using something far away. The ability to recognise what God has made available is something you need God's grace for. In the name of Jesus, I fervently pray for the opening of your eyes.

The things that God has prepared for those who love him, however, have not yet been seen by human eyes, heard by human ears, or

even entered into human hearts, as it is written.
Because the Spirit searches all things, even the deep things of God, and because no one knows the things of God except the Spirit of God, God has revealed them to us by his Spirit. 1 Corinthians 2:9–12 For we have not received the spirit of the world, but the spirit which is of God; that we might know the things which are freely given to us of God.

You'll become aware of the things that God has given you thanks to the work of the Holy Spirit.

God and Father of our Lord Jesus Christ, who has given us all spiritual blessings in heavenly regions through Christ: Ephesians 1:3.

Through knowledge of the one who has called us to glory and virtue, his divine power has given to us all things pertaining to life and godliness:
2 Peter 1:3

It all hinges on your ability to understand how to access what God has already given you rather than what you are looking for.

A trap set by the devil is planning to use what you lack for the next stage of your success. God wants us to begin with what we already have, not with what is yet to come.

In John 6, Jesus faced the difficulty of not having enough food to feed the large number of people who were with Him. He approached God with thanksgiving for what He already had and a possibility mindset; as a result, God intervened and the food became surplus.

If you don't know what to do when faced with a task, frustration is likely to result.

To succeed in life and business, you must unleash the potential that already exists inside of you.

God will always make something out of what you have. Your future success depends on what is currently available, not on what you do not yet have. In reality, hating what you have now will make your future worse. Even though what you have might not seem like enough in the material sense, God's divine grace makes what you have sufficient. Because every lifting is concealed in something, if you can think clearly enough, what you already have is sufficient to start with. Create a new mentality.

The seed you have today contains the potential for financial growth for tomorrow; if you choose not to plant that seed, you will unavoidably forfeit your harvest for tomorrow. Stop viewing life through the lens of challenges and begin viewing it through the lens of miracles. You go on to the following stage when you can recognise something. What you need is usually concealed in what you already have (Matthew 25:14–28).

One of the richest persons in the world, Bill Gates, saw the opportunity to start his firm with the $200 he had. His name is still spoken when discussing successful businesspeople.

If you want to run or win a race, you cannot skip the first step. As you move forward and achieve in business, start something with what you already have to gauge how successful you will be there. Keep in mind that "small beginnings" have power.

CHAPTER 6: HOW TO START BUSINESS WITHOUT MONEY

Consider posing the following query: "How would one start a business without money?" "Is it possible?" It is, indeed! You must sit down and make a plan if you want to get out of any circumstance.

How can he not likewise freely give us everything else if he did not spare his own Son but gave him up for us all?

Romans 8:32

God the Father is willing to grant you what your heart desires if He was able to give up His Son for our redemption. If you haven't gotten it, it only indicates you're clueless about how to acquire it.

The goal of business is to turn a profit. Capital (money) is therefore the first factor individuals take into account when beginning a business. Money shouldn't always be the first thing that comes to mind; other factors should also be taken into account; capital cannot be confined to just money. There are more resources that can be introduced into business. Your MIND, which is the capital of your life, should also be taken into account when beginning a business. What it takes to exploit is something you carry around with you constantly. Your mind is your most valuable asset because it houses your faculties for wisdom and achievement. Your future will be greater the bigger your thinking is. Starting a business might not be a good idea unless your thinking is put to use.

Don't prioritise borrowing while starting a firm. It is wise for you to avoid doing this habit, which is one that most people have. Borrowing is the act of borrowing something from someone with their consent with the intention of returning it later. Borrowing is weighty and against the scriptures!

And you must not borrow; rather, you must lend to many nations.
Deuteronomy 28:12

If God has no intention of making you a lender, He cannot tell you to lend. Borrowing has the result that you will constantly be under obligation to pay back the money to the lender. Have you ever borrowed while unwinding? God does not want you to be a borrower; rather, He wants you to be a lender in terms of His purpose for you.
Any pressure you experience, God will provide a way out for you.

God made everything he made from nothing. He used His brains, not money, to create; this is how wise he was. In His likeness, He also made humans (Genesis 1:26-27). Your mind was given to you at your new birth, and it is filled with knowledge and strength. You are a co-creator because of (1 Corinthians 2:16; 1 Corinthians 1:24). God (the Word) spoke at the moment of creation. It is an abuse of redemption for a Christian to fail because when you dedicated your life to Jesus Christ, there was a miraculous mind transplant.

The earth was constructed by the LORD through wisdom, and the heavens were built through understanding.
His wisdom causes the depths to be split, and the clouds to release their dew.
Proverbs 3 : 19-20

The universe as a whole was created by wisdom. According to the Bible, "Wisdom is the main thing." Therefore, your main asset in business endeavours is wisdom. Wisdom is the capacity to use your thinking in an efficient and productive manner. You cannot have Christ's mind and expect the world to ignore you. Even if you possess something but are unaware of it, it still might exist. It will work for you if you put some effort into it.

Your mind is the place of reasoning, which when used properly could produce a desired result. No wonder God said in Isaiah 1:18 Come now and let us reason together... Obedience to this word makes you command business exploits and live in abundance. Wealth is conceived in wisdom, so creating wealth is therefore not a function of money but of wisdom. If you can think enough, what you have is enough to start from any point. I did something when I became born again. I wasn't particularly smart in school, but once I was reborn, I developed a peculiar insight of the creative power of heaven. I started reading the book of Daniel and discovered from the Bible that Daniel was 10 times more superior than his contemporaries. I also realised that we are under a better covenant as a result of the new birth. My intellect was stimulated as a result of my purposeful self-work!

Today, I stand as a living example of God's grace; he has elevated me above my contemporaries. All praise be to God! One of our class's top students and I were chatting when he expressed his amazement at how God's knowledge had been working in my life.

You cannot be reborn while trapped, in need of funding to launch a business. You can have anything you can imagine. A man who will have an excuse for doing nothing is one who is lazy.

At the appropriate time, investing in capital might be a good decision. It's an opportunity that can provide benefits with sharp thinking and diligent work. You have the Holy Spirit within you as a Christian, thus turning to a mortal man for assistance would be extremely disobedient. You can have faith in the Holy Spirit. God has provided the Holy Spirit to us for our benefit. Corinthians 12:7. Provocative thoughts will get things moving in your head.

If not used, the thought of Christ within you will remain dormant. It's similar to having a teacup full of liquids, sugar, and water that needs to be swirled with a teaspoon before you can drink it. You set the pace on earth by challenging your intellect to produce an exceptional result.

Sources where you can raise money without taking out a loan:

1. VALUABLES

These are your priceless possessions, including your vehicles, electronics, collectibles, shoes, purses, and other valuables that aren't now in use. Instead of seeking elsewhere, collect them all, sell them, and use the proceeds to launch the business you've always wanted.

2. SAVINGS

This is yet another way to improve any business. Every child of God is required to practise saving. When you save, you give yourself time to organise your life gradually.

3. SELLING OFF PRIOR INVESTMENTS

Stock sales might be used to finance new ventures.

4. RETIREMENT ADVANTAGES

Beneficiaries are permitted to use their inheritance to launch a business once they have reached the term of gratuity or pension.

5. THE GIFTS OF WELL-WISHERS

This is money that was earned through your child's baptism, birthday party, etc. Additionally, it can be used to launch something.

6. COOPERATIVE OR JOINT VENTURE

You can start a business by collaborating with someone based on your shared love, trust, and shared ideologies.

Can two people walk together if they both agree?
Amos 3:3

Getting together with someone to launch a successful business is a fantastic idea. Make sure there is adequate documentation when you want to participate in such an agreement.

7. WASTE TO CAPITAL

Look at the pieces you have been wasting if you wish to find something in the future.

In John 6:12, Jesus mentions feeding 5,000 people. God doubled what He already had.

He made sure the fragments weren't wasted after feeding them. Why would He act that way? Why didn't He get rid of them? He was predicting the future! What you consider to be a waste could be used to launch a different enterprise. Stopped squandering! Avoid being a waster if God must sustain ongoing divine supply; you must have a life investment strategy.

Your company needs to establish a culture of diligence, excellence, accountability, and caution if it wants to enjoy a steady flow of cash. You shouldn't act carelessly just because you hit the first target; instead, put the money back into your company and exercise self-control.

CHAPTER 7: USEFUL TIPS FOR BUSINESS EXPLOITS

Each trade has its own secrets. No matter how long you work for Coca-Cola, they will never divulge their trade secrets to you. The trade secret is what gives any business its competitive edge.

Every success in the kingdom of God can be linked to a secret that was unearthed.

The LORD, our God, is the owner of the secrets, but the things that have been made public belong to us and our offspring forever

so that we may obey all the commands of this law.
Deuteronomy 29:29

It asserts that although God has hidden the things, we must find them.

As I was in my youth, when God's secret covered my tabernacle Job 29:4

God was giving Job secrets, and as a result, he rose to become the richest man in the entire East at the time. A serious businessperson is willing to complete their task and is fervently committed to it; they do not play around with their tasks.

You are not in business if you are not on a mission. God is not opposed to engaging in a legitimate business. Since Jesus Christ was a businessman while He was on Earth, He responded, "Wist ye not that I must be about my Father's business?" Luke 2:49. God cherished Abraham, a successful businessman (Genesis 12). God addressed him as His buddy since he was not slack in his business. Business should not turn you against God; rather, it should strengthen your relationship with him. Because Abraham never let his business cause him to stray from obeying God, it makes sense that God suggested in Isaiah 51:1-2 that we should imitate him.

Abraham followed specific procedures that helped him advance his business to new heights.

THE EIGHT STEPS OF ABRAHAM TO GREATER BUSINESS SUCCESS

1. RELATIONSHIP WITH GOD

Abraham had a close relationship with God
and consistently followed the will of God.
When it was all said and done, Melchizedek,
the King of Salem, realised just how closely
connected Abraham was to God and how
God had been watching over him. Abraham
had no choice but to receive the king's
recognition (Genesis 14:19–20). He might
mention Abraham as a person who interacted
with God.
You must identify with God if you want to
be at peace in your life and in your company.

Get to know him right away, and by being at
ease, pleasant things will come to you.
Job 22:21

You will become associated with successful commercial endeavours when you identify with God.

2. OBEDIENCE

Additionally, this is essential and cannot be disregarded.

You are my friends if you follow my instructions.
John 15:14

If God wants to communicate with you, you must obey him.

The LORD will reveal his covenant to those who fear him and reveal his secret to them.
Psalm 25:14

Divine mysteries can only be revealed to those who adore (fear) the Lord. Your business will prosper if you are prepared to respect and obey God.

3. VISION

Abraham had access to a divine plan and was a man of insight.

Get out of your nation, your family, and your father's house and go to a land that I will show you, the LORD had commanded Abram.
Genesis 12 : 1

Abraham became famous because he had access to the Divine programme. His fame grew as a result of his submission to divine guidance and devotion to God's commands!

You won't want to be bothered by any demon or his agents, no matter what their position, while the Lord is leading. Psalm 23:1-5

Allow God to guide you if you want to succeed; quit following what is trending.

They are the sons of God because they are all guided by the Holy Spirit.
Romans 8 :14

Give the Holy Spirit room to guide you.

4. DILIGENCE

When he was 80 years old, Abraham went to war to save Lot when he was still in the livestock business at age 75.

There is no replacement for effort if you want to achieve greatnes⁶s. Either you are exerting a lot of effort or not at all. Making a difficult life your default option is preferable to working hard.

Do you observe a person working hard at his job? He will stand in front of monarchs, not lowly people.
Proverbs 22:29

When a man is dedicated to his task, brilliance manifests itself in him.

Hard effort cannot be replaced by fasting or prayer. Avoid becoming engrafted in inactivity; refrain from saying "I have faith that God will provide" while making inactivity your companion; this is not Christianity.

Either you are a dedicated worker or a despicable beggar. Refuse to do nothing.

5. GIVING

Abraham was generous and a tither. You must be a tither in order to get Abraham's blessings. Abraham was businessman because he gave tithes, which is why. He was a man with a big heart who offered sacrifices without thinking twice. You will never succeed in business unless you are an enthusiastic and dedicated giver. Every great in the kingdom has historically been a businessman, but I have always been a giver.

6. FAITH

Abraham was a devout man. who rejected hope nonetheless held onto it. And not having a poor faith... He was strong in faith and gave praise to God, not stumbling at the promise of God because of unbelief Romans 4:18–20

You must have specific faith in God that whatever He promises to do, He can actually accomplish if you want to make business news. Whenever you find a promise in His Word and believe it, you commit Him to act in your favour.

To him, Jesus remarked, "If you can believe, all things are possible."
Mark 9:23

It is impossible to please God without faith (Hebrews 11:6). Believe in God!

7. CONTENTMENT

With what he had, Abraham was happy. Your tomorrow's blessings are guaranteed by your happiness now.

But being a godly person who is content is a big gain.
1 Timothy 6 :6

Be thankful for what God has given you and be content with it. Covetousness could prevent God from blessing you.

8. GRATITUDE

Thanking God for everything that He has done for you inspires Him to do even more.

Giving thanks to the Lord is a good thing.
Psalm 92:1

Always praise God for enabling you to succeed at every stage or phase of your business.

CHAPTER 8: OUTSTANDING CUSTOMER SERVICE

The appreciated consideration and care given to each customer before, during, or after they patronise your business is referred to as excellent customer service. The most important competitive advantage for any firm has been and will continue to be superior customer service. It was predicted by Bill

Gates that "customer service will become the primary value added function of every business." People who are excellent at business view customer service as an essential component of commercial exploitation.

Business is primarily someone's regular job, profession, or trade. It is a system of economic or organisational exchange where products and services are given or received in exchange for money. Making a profit is only one aspect of business; another is making sure the consumer is taken care of, even if doing so costs money. Any legitimate trade of products and services with the goal of putting the needs of the consumer ahead of making a profit is considered this. John Mackey Said:

"Our consumers are our most crucial stakeholder, not our stockholders, for us. Our primary goal as a company is to fulfil the needs and preferences of our main clientele. The term "customer" can also refer to a client or a purchaser. A client is someone who purchases goods, services, or other items from a seller, vendor, or provider in exchange for money or another form of value.

The customer is still at the centre of any successful firm. He sets the direction for the company, determining whether it will continue to be successful or fail. Any company that is unable to keep up a positive rapport with its clients will cease to exist. If you defraud a customer, your firm will lose future revenue. If you treat a consumer rudely or carelessly, your business will suffer.

Most individuals are aware of the rules for living a successful life, but few actually follow them. It is more advantageous to act on what you know rather than merely knowing something.

Happy are you if you follow these instructions if you know them.
John 13:17

The main goal of business is to persuade a customer to refer to other customers. It goes beyond just turning a profit. It is all about retaining clients and ensuring their contentment. Don't enter into business with the intention of taking advantage of your consumers; doing so could have a negative impact on both you and your company. It can threaten your future and put an end to your company. The majority of business owners believe that economic collapse, poor public policy, high taxes, or ineffective advertising tactics are to blame for their company's loss. A disgruntled or unfairly treated consumer may be more essential than all these factors together. Your most dissatisfied clients are your biggest source of learning, according to Bill Gates. Give your company a superior customer relationship approach if you want it to succeed.

As a businessperson, your greatest asset is not your inventory of goods, services, or real estate; rather, it is your customer base, as without them, you would not be in operation.

There is only one boss, according to Wal-Mart founder Sam Walton: the customer. Do not underestimate the power of a customer in your commercial contacts with him or her. He or she can dismiss everyone in the firm, from the chairman on down, by just spending his money somewhere else.

The passage is found in Proverbs 29:18. Where there is no vision, the people perish. While vision is key in business, wisdom is just as critical for realising your goals. But wisdom is advantageous to direct, the Bible stated. 10:10 in Ecclesiastes. Always be wise in how you interact with consumers because without people (customers), a vision cannot survive.

The key to any business' success is providing excellent customer service. As a businessperson or woman, your goal should be to make sure that every customer leaves happy and satisfied with their experience. They will recommend them to other potential consumers, who will then keep coming back. Your consumers are interested in how much care you have for them, not how knowledgeable you are in that field or what you own.

Depending on how each of your customers feels after doing business with you, they could either help or hurt your company.

Jesus carried out His work (preaching the gospel, in this case) while He was still on earth with excellence and achieved great success. Luke 2:49 Today, His work has reached every corner of the globe, and He is continually winning lives to His kingdom! As an illustration, consider what Jesus accomplished in John 4:27–42. By the well, He spoke with a Samaritan lady and offered her His creation—the Word. She was completely persuaded when he divulged to her some of her personal secrets. She told everyone she could of her satisfaction, and by doing so, she led many people to Jesus.

The Gentiles then requested that these words
be delivered to them on the following
Sabbath after the Jews had left the
synagogue.
And on the following sabbath day, nearly the
entire city gathered to hear the message of
God.
Acts 13:42,44

The people received an excellent message
and asked for more. As a result, the multitude
of people (customers) increased. A pastor's
ministry is similar to customer service in that
it is necessary for a church to expand.

Before, during, or after doing business with
you, every customer is continually seeking
out a great or fulfilling relationship. Any
company that does not appear to be pleasant
to its customers will undoubtedly fail. You

cannot succeed in business if you lack the ability to care.

Each client expects two key things from you as a businessperson:

1. What you say and do to him before, during, and after he gives you money.

2. What you say prior to, during, and following his favour.

CERTAIN WAYS TO IMPLY THAT YOU CARE ABOUT YOUR CUSTOMERS

1. ANSWER YOUR PHONE CALLS

He shall call upon me, and I will answer him.
Psalm 91:15

Call unto me, and I will answer thee...
Jeremiah 33:3

God takes your calls and responds. Learn to answer calls so you can conduct business. Purchase a phone answering system and hire staff to handle it. When someone calls to ask questions, be sure they are speaking on the phone. Keep in mind that a displeased caller will likely become a displeased customer and may go to another competitor. Customers prefer to speak with live people rather than a machine that will never be able to provide the information they seek. Avoid utilising recorded false robot calls to answer the phone. It's critical to realise that a customer's first impression of your business will be based on how you answer the phone for your company or place of business.

HOW TO ANSWER PHONE CALLS CORRECTLY

I. Respond to phone calls before the third ring.

II. When you speak with warm eagerness,

Iii. Extend a sincere welcome to the caller.

IV. Give your name and your organisation. In order for your caller to understand you, speak slowly and clearly.

V. Avoid using a stammerer to answer the phone because it can be extremely frustrating and upsetting since the caller could not know him.

Vi. Abstain from utilising slang when returning calls. Use phrases like "certainly very well" instead of okay.

VII. When I answer a phone, I am confident. Say let me find out instead of I don't know.

VIII. Read phone messages carefully and ask questions if you don't understand anything. or surnames, ask the caller to repeat or spell it for you if you are unable to spell it.

IX. Before putting a caller on wait, make sure to get their permission. After no more than 40 seconds, inform the caller of the status.I promise to get in touch with you again; please know that I still want to.

X. If a call is private or secret and intended just for one person, avoid putting the caller on speaker mode.

XI. Ensure that everyone in your company or organisation answers calls in the same way by using the advice I just gave.

2. DON'T FORGET TO BUDGET FOR A REPLACEMENT OR REFUND. POLICIES FOR RECALLS

Then they said, "We'll restore them and won't ask anything of them."
Nehemiah 5:12

If a company does not have a consumer refund, replacement, and recall policy in the event that the owner makes a mistake, that company will quickly go out of business. Customers don't want perfection from you, only that you respond to their complaints by making changes. You should be worried about the consumers' reactions if they give you a job. Every consumer seeks a remedy to an issue brought on by a product purchased or service received. Keep in mind that no customer is ready to waste money on subpar goods and services.

If a company does not have a consumer refund, replacement, and recall policy in the event that the owner makes a mistake, that company will quickly go out of business. Customers don't want perfection from you, only that you respond to their complaints by making changes. You should be worried about the consumers' reactions if they give you a job. Every consumer seeks a remedy to an issue brought on by a product purchased or service received. Keep in mind that no customer is ready to waste money on subpar goods and services.

3. PAY ATTENTION TO A CUSTOMER'S GRIEVANCE.

Don't ignore it if a consumer complains about the service provided (in relation to the things you sold him). Analyse it attentively and start making changes right away.

Because of this, the LORD of hosts says, "Consider your ways."
Haggai 1:5

The client is always right; you must respect him and refrain from arguing. To listen to him in a debate over a disgruntled client is to lose that customer to a rival business. The most significant visitor to a business, according to Mahatma Gandhi, is a client. We are reliant on him; he is not reliant on us. He is not a distraction from our work; rather, he serves as its goal and is not an outsider to our business. He is involved with it. Serving him benefits both of us; we are not giving him a favour.

The consumer is the most crucial component of every organisation. Your business won't be successful without the consumer. Your company will only achieve significant success if your clients are pleased and satisfied. Making it simple for clients to contact you can help you learn about their issues and address them. Think of their concerns as a way for you to get feedback so you can get better.

IMPORTANT ADVICE FOR HANDLING CUSTOMERS' COMPLAINTS

Regardless of the nature of the complaint or the customer's response, maintain the highest level of professionalism and composure.

Make sure you understand the issue completely by asking questions. Even though you may not believe it is your fault at that point, you provide remedies.

convey gratitude for their telling you and convey compassion for their inconvenience. If you made a mistake, be sure to accept responsibility for it.

Within a given time frame, present solutions to their issues or concerns, and make sure you don't let them down to avoid losing their trust.

A few days later, follow up the complaint with a call or email. This demonstrates your sincerity in attempting to solve the issue.

Teach your employees and yourself to treat customers with decency and politeness.

Customer service is more than simply a department; it encompasses every employer and employee assessment that is handled, starting at the entrance. The quality of the company's customer service and how impressed you are will depend on how you act in the office. As a result, everyone needs to understand customer service. A rude approach towards consumers can result in the business suffering unthinkable losses. As the company's leader, make sure to provide customer service training for your workers. The morale of potential customers can be destroyed, your client relationships can be strained, and your business might be destroyed by untrained personnel.Rudeness is the weak person's attempt to appear strong. When employees treat customers with snobbery, customers will start to think poorly of the company. Politeness, according to former American president Theodore Roosevelt, is a show of dignity, not servitude. Your business relationship with a consumer will be strengthened when you are courteous to them (in speech or deed).

During His time on earth, Jesus spent three and a half years teaching His followers the basics of customer service. As they put what they had learned into practice, the church flourished and became exceedingly powerful. The physical body of Jesus Christ is still in charge today.

According to statistics, more than 40% of consumers who switched banks did so as a result of the staff's poor demeanour, rudeness, and lack of consideration for them. Be careful how you interact with your customers. There are certain comments you should avoid making in their presence. Successful. Making a customer happy is doing everything possible to earn their business and their referral of goods and services to others.

God did not intend for you to fail. He is the most prosperous God, and He has imbued you with His capacity. You contain all you require for success.

Most people struggle because they lack action but know too much. Principles by themselves do not make you great; application does.

HOW TO RELATE WITH CUSTOMERS

[ ] CREATE A POSITIVE MINDSET

Never underestimate the damage that a negative attitude may cause. When each letter is compared to its corresponding number, the word ATTITUDE sums to 100%. In other words, A=1, T=20, T=20, I=9, T=20, U=21, D=4, and E=5 add up to 100. Consequently, Do Outstandingly well in business.

Customers must be treated with a positive attitude at all times. It affects whether or not your business will advance. Customers may stop supporting a business for a variety of reasons, but poor customer service is the only factor in these occurrences. Death accounted for 1% of resignations, company relocation accounted for 3%, relocation caused 5% of resignations, product dissatisfaction accounted for 7% of resignations, and attitude indifference by management or staff accounted for 84% of resignations.

[ ] DEVELOP RESPECT

You need your customers, therefore don't deceive or lie to them. Maintaining your current clientele is far simpler than acquiring new ones. Be kind to the people you already have.

[ ] KNOW WHAT YOUR CUSTOMERS WANT.

Understanding your customers' requirements and expectations is absolutely necessary for providing excellent customer service. Always operate with a feedback system.

[ ] BE GRATEFUL TO THEM.

Get their complete details and express your appreciation for their business.

[ ] KEEP ENHANCING.

What might be fashionable today might be outdated tomorrow! Continue to do better and, if necessary, issue refunds for all complaints. Every unhappy customer will tell others about their experience, so be sure to keep getting better.

A FEW IMPORTANT TIPS FOR GREAT CUSTOMER SERVICE

[ ] LOVE YOURSELF LIKE YOU LOVE YOUR CUSTOMERS.

Love encourages concern; when you love someone, you want them to be comfortable. Serving people and attending to their needs is one way to demonstrate your love for them.

Don't just focus on your own things; consider other people's things as well.
Philippians 2:4

A business approach that can improve the performance of your organisation and support her development for the future is loving your customers. If you value your clients, they will return frequently and recommend you to others.

[ ] PUT PEOPLE FIRST BEFORE PROFIT.

Profit should not take the place of People because it is the customer that brings profit. The absence of a customer is the absence of business and consequently; no profit. If you place people before profit, the people will bring the profit but if you place profit before people, when they get, there will be no profit.

[ ] TREAT YOUR CLIENTS THE WAY YOU WANT TO BE TREATED.

In light of this, treat others the same way you would like to be treated.
Matthew 7:12

If you value yourself and your company highly, you should also value your clients highly. Make sure your business creates a thoughtful and consistent customer policy. It will help you win a lot of business. Respect others if you want them to respect you.

It is wise for a pastor to be able to communicate with the congregation effectively so as to avoid alienating them; keep in mind that they are God's people, not yours. Don't let your annoying attitude mar God's plans.

[ ] ALWAYS PROVIDE YOUR CLIENTS WITH MORE SERVICES AND ATTENTION THAN THEY ANTICIPATED.

God Himself is an expert at going above and beyond what people want or anticipate.

Now to him who is capable of doing far more than all of our requests or thoughts combined...
Ephesians 3:20

When you give someone more than they anticipate, they will undoubtedly return.

Because Joseph gave more to pharaoh than he had asked for, he was appointed as prime minister. He was summoned by Pharaoh to interpret the dream, but after instructing him on food preservation techniques, he was appointed Prime Minister.

Giving your clients more than they expect from you leaves a lasting impression on them and encourages them to use your services again.

While hatred repels people, acceptance draws them in. Even more harm than you might think could be done to you by one hostile customer. The importance of customer service demands that you and your staff uphold it. The business is not monopolised by you.

[ ] NEVER LET A COMPLAINT GO UNATTENDED

In response to concerns, be proactive in seeking solutions; pay attention to issues and make an effort to address them.

[ ] PAY YOUR CLIENTS IMMEDIATE ATTENTION.

Nobody has time to squander, so refrain from conversing with your coworkers while customers are waiting.

[ ] RESPECT YOUR PRODUCT WARRANTY AND KEEP YOUR WORD!

A customer's confidence in your goods and services is increased by elements like dependability and integrity. It is the key to retaining customers and gaining their business again and again. The same principle holds true for a customer's appointments and due dates. A failed promise might damage your estimations and reflect poorly on your company. Nothing makes clients more uneasy. Your business is ruled by your words and promises.

With the words that come out of your mouth, you catch yourself and are captured.
Proverbs 6:2

Never make a customer a promise that you know you won't be able to fulfil. Customers no longer trust you. Never put off any delivery intended for you or your clients because they might find someone else. Your customer will think you are dishonest if you decline to deliver the product you promised. A good reputation is preferable to having all the wealth in the world.

A GOOD name should always be preferred over huge wealth, and loving favour over cash and gold.
Proverbs 22 :1

Integrity safeguards any company for a prosperous future. Do not assume that just because you are at the top now, you will stay there if you don't provide good customer service.

1. CUSTOMERS SHOULD RECEIVE THE SAME LEVEL OF SERVICE

whether they are filing a complaint or returning an item. When a customer returns a product they're not happy with, treat them with the same decency and respect. Your relationship with them will improve if you pay attention to the complaint and make changes. Your company will flourish and make money thanks to it. Even some businesses have the phrase "Anything bought here must never be returned" printed on their receipts. Because you are allowed to return something you buy if a flaw is found in them, it is not an international commercial norm.

2. NEVER PERMIT AN ANGRY OR DISSATISFIED CONSUMER TO DEPART

To ensure that they will always return, do all in your power to make them happy before they depart. Ten people could hear about your rudeness from one disgruntled customer. With your customers, stay out of pointless disputes. Allow your clients to make mistakes; yet, if you can't, reprimand them politely and with high regard. Do not scold or belittle them. In an organisation, the customer is the most crucial figure. Shareholders would not have anything to share if the client didn't exist.

A gentle response deflects fury, while painful words inflame rage.
Proverbs 15 :1

If you treat them like a king, they will come back; yet, if you treat them like slaves, they won't.

3. ALWAYS TELL YOUR CUSTOMERS THE TRUTH

ABOUT THE PRODUCTS AND SERVICES

When they trust your information, they will keep coming to patronize you and amend your productS to others. Do not lie to your customer about your product,

THE FOUNDATION OF SUCCESSFUL CUSTOMER CARE IS FORMED BY FIVE ETHICAL BUSINESS QUALITIES.

These characteristics serve as the foundation for all other customer service values. Until you understand how to care for people, you can study all the principles and still not become a principal.

1. TRUSTWORTHINESS

One of the best values you can give any consumer is this. When it comes to being dependable, you don't need the client to remind you to fulfil your commitments and carry out what you have stated.

Showing yourself to be an example of good deeds in all you do, including your doctrine, is important.
Titus 2:7

Show integrity in your dealings so that people will regard what you say as a genuine statement of your beliefs and intentions.

2. INTEGRITY

This is the quality that best characterises a whole person or organisation. He is a person who is unwavering and acts in accordance with his principles rather than what he observes at any given time. It entails operating according to principles rather than circumstances.

Let me be protected by my honesty and integrity...
Psalm 25:21

Integrity must be maintained.

3. LOYALTY

This is a commitment to the client to ensure that the goods and services are provided to them in a manner that meets their needs. Customers who are loyal to you feel valued, honoured, and like they are in control of the deal.

The days have come, declares the LORD, when I will fulfil the excellent promise I made to the house of Israel and the house of Judah.

Isaiah 33:14

You have no purpose in providing the services and justifications you have promised if God is committed to keeping His word to His people. To continue doing business, you must do this.

4. ACCOUNTABILITY

The best way to gauge customer service is through this. Businesses and organisations that are prepared to remain relevant learn to accept responsibility for activities that fall short of what customers anticipate.

5. FAIRNESS

To make sure that every action taken to take care of a customer is something that affects everyone, this is done. When interacting with customers, avoid being biassed or showing favouritism.

Every customer service should be built on these fundamental principles. The foundation of care is not wasted effort. Every business that wishes to endure must practise care.

ESSENTIAL CAUSES FOR CUSTOMER CARE

1. It shows people that you really care about them. Customers will listen to what you say but will believe what you do.

2. It gives you and your team a source of pride and confidence.

3. It serves as a contributing factor for business growth.

4. It virtually eliminates competition. When you please them, you stand above others of the same interest.

SOME PRACTICAL THINGS ABOUT CUSTOMER CARE

1. PAY ATTENTION TO YOUR CLIENT

Learn to pay attention to your customers and modify your offerings to suit their needs. If you don't pay attention and give them a chance to speak, you can offer a personal opinion that won't satisfy the client.

2. ADDRESS THE COMPLAINT

Any consumer who bravely criticises your goods and services is a customer willing to return if they are pleased.

3. INFORM CLIENTS ABOUT YOUR GOODS AND SERVICES.

Continue to remind them that some products and services have changed. Regular communication gives customers the impression that they are significant and always relevant to your products and services. Inform them about your new offerings in a mail. Give them updates about your goods, whether it's about new products or a price change. Keep a list of every person you do business with.

4. ACTIVATE THE DISABLED

Never relate to customers with an emphasis on their disabilities. Some locations aren't made to accommodate people in wheelchairs. Such individuals should be accommodated by every company. Your business's advertisement gains more traction when a disabled customer is satisfied.

5. GIVE A LITTLE MORE

Every man is a friend to the giver of gifts, and many will seek the prince's favour.
Proverbs 19:6

Whatever the size, give your consumers a gift. Nobody does not value getting something more in addition to what they have paid for. Buy gifts for all of your loyal customers at the end of the year. The paradox of good customer service is that it eventually generates more fresh promotions than can be accomplished by millions of commercials and partnerships. The best strategy for advertising a firm is through customer service.

CHAPTER 9: ACHIEVE PROGRESS

Genesis Chapter One's narrative provides a clear description of progression. God progressed via various tiers. He did not produce everything in a single day. The similar strategy can be used in business. As you progress from one level to the next, your company success becomes clear. There should be progress rather than staying where you "started" in the beginning. Jesus had a beginning as well. In chapter two of the Book of John, he also used the same illustration. Learn to start with what you have right now if you want to succeed. Think large from the outset, but work with what you have, and keep moving forward.

Most people struggle with the problem of starting out big but eventually disappointing God's plan for their lives.

Who has overlooked the day of little things?
Zechariah 4:10

Even though you started out tiny, you should eventually grow significantly.
Job 8:7

To hate the times of humble beginnings is to hate your future. Although it is generally loathed, being little actually serves as the foundation for greatness. You might be prevented from progressing if you ignore the law of progression. Start with what you have; this is not a sign of uncertainty but rather of preparation. Planning cannot be replaced by faith. The All-Powerful God had to make a plan, and if He, to whom everything is possible, changed course, then you are not exempt. The most reliable technique to climb a mountain is one step at a time. Each lengthy trip begins with a single step.

Failure to take the initial step will result in failure to reach your goal.

Most millionaires started off in small businesses with modest beginnings. For instance, the hamburger chain MacDonald's began as a small operation and has since expanded globally. CNN is viewed worldwide today, but Ted Turner launched the network in a single room. The Coca-Cola beverage began modestly but is now well known throughout the world.

You won't succeed in business if you don't adhere to the progressional idea. You will get more stable as you proceed from one step to the next. You won't have an orange tree if I hate an orange seed. Get to become an adult because no child is born as one. The current state of his development is sufficient to begin your next miracle.

God worked a miracle using the rod that Moses was holding. God would never make an effort to multiply what you lack. Being too arrogant to start small is a disguised form of self-deception, so try to avoid it. Do all you can from where you are and with what you have, and then put the rest in God's hands. What you already have has the ability to set what you're looking for in motion. Stars of the world are men of motion. Starting small offers you a solid foundation and helps you feel more certain that you can succeed.

Looking to Jesus, the founder and perfecter of our faith, who, for the joy given to him,

bore the cross while shunning the shame and has been seated at the right hand of God's throne.
Hebrew 12:2

Jesus never saw His own humiliation and punishment as a roadblock to the realisation of His goals, but rather as a bridge.

Always see the future by placing a visual in front of you, allowing yourself to feature it, and starting to see it. You can see where you are headed when you start out tiny, so you don't become upset by what happens. Be confident and avoid feeling embarrassed.

IMPROVE YOUR TERRITORY SIZE

The narrative of Jabez in First Chronicles chapter four serves as evidence that what matters most is not who you are or what your parents had in mind for you, but rather who you plan to be and what you ask for, regardless of the situation. God bless you, regardless of your background or level of poverty. Even when everything seems hopeless, you can transform your future with a simple, faith-filled prayer.

Ask. and it will be yours; look, and you will see; knock. and it will be unlocked for you: Matthew 7:7

Asking in faith will enable you to modify your circumstances at any time. God is impartial; if you ask Him for something, He will also give it to you because He has no regard for anyone.

Jabez just spoke the phrase "Oh that you would increase my territory." He want more accountability so that he might leave his mark for God. Jabez went to the God of heaven rather than any man for a blessing.

And everything you ask for in prayer, with faith, you will receive.
Matthew 21:22

Be sure to bless me with an awareness of enlargement as you say it. You pray to God for growth in your marriage, business, and investment.

In the name of Jesus, you will receive everything your heart desires.

BENEFITS OF PROGRESSIVE POWER

[ ] YOU ENJOY SEEING DEVELOPMENT.

Starting small ensures that you'll make progress over time, which makes you happy and causes you to become thrilled.

[ ] THROUGH LIFE'S PROCESS, YOU BECOME MORE STABLE.

Every stage is a stable stage because stability comes from advancement.

[ ] YOU HAVE THE CHANCE TO GROW MENTALLY AND TAKE ON CHALLENGES.

Business challenges push you to your limits. The challenge's benefit is that it increases your ability to execute. It challenges you to take on giants and prevail.

[ ] YOU LEARN HUMILITY THROUGH IT

You must be modest if you want to succeed in business. A man who advances should never be proud.

[ ] IT ENSURES UPCOMING DISCIPLINE

When they were full, he instructed his followers to gather the leftover pieces so that nothing would be lost.
John 6:12

When you develop gradually, you will never waste anything.

[ ] YOU RECEIVE EXPERIENCE AS A RESULT.

You cannot succeed in big business until you beat small business. When you have not tackled modest problems, you become afraid of huge challenges.

[ ] YOU DEFEAT INACTIVITY.

Getting started slowly requires action. You can reach your objective if you start small and have huge dreams in mind. The challenges you are currently confronting won't terrify you if you can see where you're headed.

THE HIDDEN PATH TO
BUSINESS SUCCESS

Ignorance is the most aggravating thing in business. Light dominates darkness, making it superior to it.

I provide the reader of this amazing book a special chance to rule in business and advance where others are stumbling.

The most important thing is wisdom (Proverbs 4:7). A kingdom dream, diligence, faithfulness, being knowledgeable, and making use of the resources available are all wise ways to run your business. Stars in both life and business are made by revealed secrets. You will learn how to establish a business without money as well as some practical advice for business ventures in this ground-breaking book.